ALEXANDER GRAHAM
BELL

Richard Tames

FRANKLIN WATTS
LONDON•SYDNEY

Contents

This edition 2003

Franklin Watts
96 Leonard Street
London
EC2A 4XD

Franklin Watts Australia
45-51 Huntley Street
Alexandria, NSW 2015

© Franklin Watts 1990, 2003

Series Editor: Hazel Poole
Editor: Dee Turner
Designer: Nick Cannan

A CIP catalogue record for this book is
available from the British Library.

ISBN 0 7496 5026 5

Printed in Belgium

In Father's Footsteps

If ever a family had the right surname, it was the Bell family. When we think of a bell, we think of it making a loud clear sound — and Alexander Graham Bell devoted his life to the study of sound, as his father and grandfather had done before him. As the inventor of the telephone, Bell's surname is particularly appropriate.

He was born in Edinburgh in 1847 and given the name Alexander. Only when he was eleven did he add the name "Graham" — because he liked it. It must have avoided confusion, too, for both his father and grandfather were also called Alexander.

Grandfather Alexander Bell (1790–1865), a firm believer in education and effort. Left: 13 South Charlotte Street, Edinburgh, Bell's birthplace.

His grandfather, Alexander Bell, was a Scottish shoemaker who had become an actor and later opened a school in London. There he taught elocution (the art of speaking) and helped people cure their speech problems, such as stammering. Alexander Bell's son, Alexander Melville Bell, carried on the family business and began a scientific study of sound at Edinburgh and London universities. As a result of these studies he invented a system of **symbols** which he called Visible Speech. Using this system it was possible to write down the sounds we

Bell's parents — Alexander Melville and Eliza Grace — who were married for fifty-two years.

make when we talk, rather in the way musical symbols allow us to record on paper the sounds made by notes of music.

In the Visible Speech system, each symbol showed how the tongue, teeth, **larynx** and lips were used to make a particular sound. This was very useful in helping people with speech problems, especially the deaf and those who tried to teach them. Until this time, most children born deaf remained dumb (unable to speak) all their lives. Now a teacher could use the symbols to "show" pupils how to make each sound.

Melville's Visible Speech system, and his many books, made him a well-known international expert on speech. His son, Alexander Graham Bell, never thought of any career but following in the footsteps of his father and grandfather. He was particularly interested in the problems of the deaf, for his own mother had been deaf since childhood. By the time he was fifteen he was already helping his father by giving public demonstrations of the Visible Speech system. A year later he and his older brother, Melly, took up their father's challenge to build an artificial "talking head". This they did, using speaking parts made from a tin tube, sheets of rubber and the larynx of a dead lamb! By blowing through it they could make it say "Mama!" Graham also learned

This page of "Visible Speech" shows a vocabulary test, including variant pronunciations by Irish, Americans, Scots and Cockneys.

(Sc.) (Sc.) (F.) (Sc.) (Sc.) (Sc.) (Am.) (Sc.) (Sc.) (Sc.) (Sc.) (Sc.) (Ga.) (Sc.) (Sc.) (Sc.) (Port.) (Sc.) (Sc.) (Sc.) (Sc.)

Hermann von Helmholtz. The German's book *On the Sensations of Tone* described how he had managed to produce artificial vowel sounds using **tuning forks** and electricity. Graham didn't know anything about electricity, and he didn't know much German either. He read the book, but could not understand it all. He mistakenly thought Helmholtz had transmitted the vowel sounds through an electric wire, the way Morse code is sent through a **telegraph**. He hadn't, but Graham's mistake turned his thoughts in a new direction. He began to consider the idea of sending sound over distance by means of electricity.

At the age of twenty, Graham went to study and teach at a college in Bath. While he was away from the family his younger brother, Edward, died of **tuberculosis**. Graham came back to London to be with his distressed family. For the next three years he assisted his father in the teaching of Visible Speech and studied part-time at University College, London. There he studied the way the human throat, mouth and ear work together to produce speech.

In May 1870, Graham's elder brother, Melly, also died of tuberculosis. The family was stunned by this second cruel blow. Graham himself began to suffer

how to press his pet dog's vocal chords to make it say "How are you, Grandmama?" — or, at least, it sounded something a bit like that.

When he was sixteen, Graham became a student teacher at Weston House, a boys school at Elgin in northern Scotland. He taught music and elocution and in return received free lessons in other subjects. He also began to make experiments to find out how different positions of the mouth and tongue combine to make the various **vowel** sounds.

Melville Bell was impressed by his son's work and showed the results to Alexander J. Ellis, an expert on language. Ellis suggested that Graham should read about the experiments of a German scientist,

terrible headaches, which would be a curse to him throughout most of his life. Fearing that his last surviving son might also sicken and die, Melville Bell took a bold step. He decided to take the surviving family away from smoky London to live in the brisk climate of Canada. The Bell family arrived in Quebec on 1 August and shortly afterwards settled in Brantford, a small town not far from Niagara Falls.

Young "Aleck" and his younger brother "Ted", whose death brought Bell back to London. Below: **Helmholtz's tuning-fork sounder. Bell confused its ability to *generate* sounds with an ability to *transmit* them.**

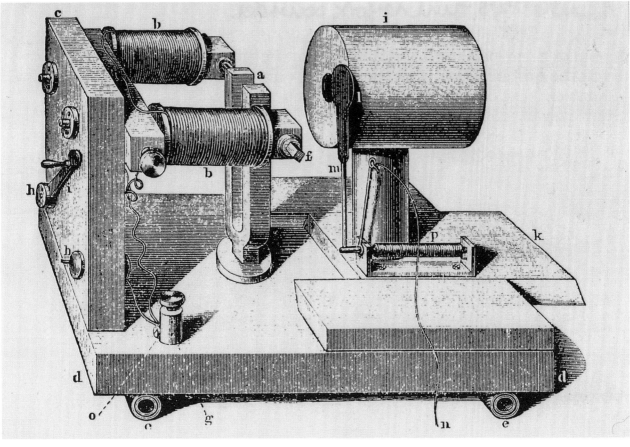

Electric Messages

The word "telephone" means "sound over a long distance". Bell is accepted as the inventor of the first successful telephone — a machine for transmitting spoken messages over a distance, using electricity. But there were other, earlier, attempts to do so.

In 1860, a German schoolteacher called Johann Philip Reis gave a public demonstration of another early telephone. This one was made from unlikely parts: a violin case, a sausage-skin, and the bung from a wooden barrel! In 1861 he showed an improved model to scientists in Frankfurt. Reis sang to his audience, while listeners gathered to receive the transmitted songs in a building about 90m (300 ft) away. Some listeners claimed they could recognize the tunes. It seems, however, that his design for a telephone was not reliable and gave poor-quality sound. Reis thought of it more as a toy, and did not **patent** it or try to make money from it. Some people were later to claim that Reis was the first inventor of the telephone, not Bell. None of these claims was upheld in a court of law, however.

Philip Reis (above) **and his musical telephone — just a curiosity rather than a new technology.**

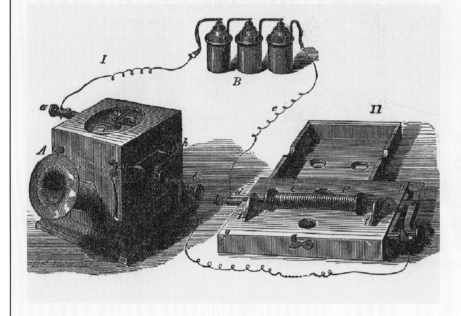

Searching for Sound

The Bell family's decision to move to North America was no leap in the dark. Bell's father was already known there as a teacher of the deaf and an expert on language. In 1868, two years before emigrating, he had gone on a lecture tour of the United States. As a result of a talk he had given in Boston, a special day school for the deaf had been set up there.

The Principal of the school, hearing that the Bells were living in Canada, wrote and invited Melville to show her teachers how to use the Visible Speech system. Instead, Melville sent his son Graham, who was now 24 years old and had been his father's full partner for two years. So, in 1871, Alexander Graham Bell moved to the United States to work in Boston. Within a few months he had improved the Visible Speech system so that it became the standard method for teaching the deaf to talk.

Boston School for the Deaf, 1871. Alexander Graham Bell is at the top of the steps on the right.

Bell then went on to teach at two other schools for the deaf. By helping deaf people to learn to speak, rather than rely on **sign language**, he allowed them to communicate more easily with hearing people.

In October 1872 Bell began to teach private pupils in his lodgings in Boston. The following year he was made a professor at the local university. Now he was successful in his own right. But he was also ambitious and wanted fortune as well as fame. He had not forgotten Helmholtz's experiments with electricity and now he had both the time and the money to spare for making experiments of his own.

Bell's original plan was to invent a

Two of Bell's deaf pupils — George Sanders and Mabel Hubbard.

"harmonic telegraph". This was a device which could recognize different musical notes. It could be made to "read" several messages transmitted at the same time along a single wire. This would greatly increase the amount of information the telegraph system could handle at any one time, so it would be cheaper to send messages.

His work as a teacher of the deaf began to put him in touch with businessmen who would become his helpers and financial backers. One of these was Thomas Sanders, a leather dealer, who was the father of one of Bell's deaf pupils. Bell's careful teaching of the five-year-old boy, George Sanders, set him on the road to speech. In October 1873 George's grateful father invited Bell to live with his family at Salem, north of Boston. Bell stayed at the Sanders' home for the next two years.

Bell also got to know Gardiner Greene Hubbard, a lawyer and president of one of the schools for the deaf where Bell had taught. Hubbard's daughter, Mabel, had caught **scarlet fever** at the age of four and was deaf as a result. Mabel also became one of Bell's pupils, though at first the fifteen-year-old girl was anything but impressed by her teacher:–

"I did not like him. He was tall and dark, with jet-black hair and eyes, but dressed badly and carelessly … he seemed hardly a gentleman."

Despite this unpromising beginning, she later married him, and they were very happily married for 45 years.

Bell's attempts to invent a harmonic telegraph led him off in another direction — the invention of a "phonautograph". This device could pick up sounds and turn them into written patterns. The idea was that it would be useful in training the deaf. They could use it to practise making different sounds and then check their progress. The patterns produced by the voice could be checked against the "correct" version, so that a deaf person could adjust the sound of his or her voice, even though they could not hear it properly.

During the summer of 1874, while staying with his parents at Brantford , Bell developed a new phonautograph. The part that responded to sound was made from the ear of a dead man.

Bell was puzzled that a tiny **membrane** in the human ear — the ear drum — could vibrate powerfully enough to move the solid bones which made up the ear's mechanism. Perhaps, he wondered, a similar membrane could be used to control the flow of an electric current in response to the air waves made by sound. This insight was the breakthrough that made the invention of the telephone possible.

A French engraving of Bell's early "ear machine".

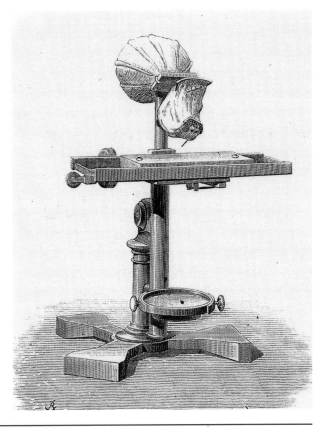

An Accidental Discovery

Sanders and Hubbard, meanwhile, were eager to keep Bell's work moving along more profitable lines. Hubbard, a lawyer, searched through the **Patent Office** files in Washington to make sure no-one else had invented anything like the harmonic telegraph. Satisfied that Bell was inventing something new, he offered him money to finance further experiments. In return he wanted a share in the profits made by any future invention. Sanders, too, proved eager to back Bell.

In February 1875, Bell, Sanders and Hubbard founded the Bell Patent Association, pledging themselves to share equally in the success of Bell's work. But they did not agree about what Bell should work on. Sanders and Hubbard wanted him to work on a harmonic telegraph, which could be turned to

immediate commercial use. But Bell was increasingly fascinated by the idea of inventing something that would make dot-dash Morse code messages obsolete by transmitting the human voice direct — a telephone.

By now Bell was conducting his experiments at an electrical shop owned by Charles Williams at 109 Court Street, Boston. He could afford to pay a skilled young technician, Thomas A. Watson, to assist him. Watson also had another useful asset: unusually good hearing. Bell needed all the help he could get, because he found out that someone else was working on the idea of a harmonic telegraph — Elisha Gray of Chicago. Gray was an expert electrician and co-founder of the Western Electric Company. Bell realized that it was "a neck and neck race between Mr Gray and myself who shall complete an apparatus first."

In March 1875, Bell went to Washington to meet Joseph Henry, a world-famous scientist and the secretary of the Smithsonian Institution. Bell showed him what he had achieved so far and asked for advice. Should he publish what he had done and let others complete the work? Or should he carry on

A Morse transmitter in operation. By the time of Bell's experiments this well-established technology was a quarter of a century old.

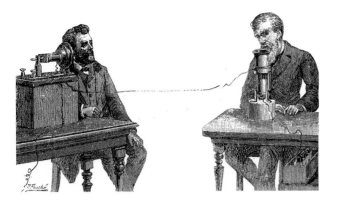

An artist's fantasy shows Bell and Gray conversing via their two very different inventions. Problems of technical incompatibility are ignored!

experimenting with it himself? Henry assured Bell that he had already produced "the germ of a great invention" and urged him to drop everything else and press on. Bell protested that he really didn't have enough knowledge of electricity. Henry's reply was simple. "Get it!" he ordered.

Henry's enthusiasm gave Bell a new confidence. He decided to abandon the race with Gray and focus his attempts on making a telephone. So he sent away all his pupils except Sanders' son. This immediately plunged him into poverty and by June he was having to borrow small sums of money from his assistant, Watson. Hubbard, dismayed at Bell's loss of interest in the harmonic telegraph, pleaded with him to abandon the telephone project. But Bell remained convinced that he was on the verge of success.

On 2 June 1875, Bell made a final breakthrough — by accident. He and Watson were working in two separate rooms on the top floor of 109 Court Street. They were testing a version of the harmonic telegraph apparatus. Bell had a transmitter in his room and a set of receivers.

Watson had receivers in his room. As usual they were having problems translating theory into practice.

In his room, Bell pressed the key which set a transmitting reed vibrating at its carefully tuned pitch. In theory the note should have been passed electrically to the receiver in Watson's room. But Watson's receiving reed did not respond. Bell wondered if this was because the reed had become stuck to the electromagnet, so he told Watson to try freeing it by plucking it with his finger. When Watson did so, he heard Bell's triumphant shout from the other room. Bell had seen the equivalent reed in his room vibrate in unison with the plucked reed. The vibrations had been passed electrically, and Bell had worked out how it had happened!

Watson's receiver had become a transmitter, due to the magnetism remaining in the electromagnet. The process was helped by Watson touching the reed with his finger. In failing to perfect the harmonic telegraph, Bell had invented a way of transmitting sound electrically — the basic principle of the telephone. That night he wrote to Hubbard in haste and excitement:–

"I have accidentally made a discovery of the very greatest importance."

The Smithsonian Institution

The Smithsonian Institution was set up in the United States, in Washington DC, in 1846. It was built using money left by the English scientist James Smithson (1765–1829). The Institution was set up as a place of learning, where knowledge could be increased and shared. Its first director was one of America's most brilliant scientists: Joseph Henry (1797–1878). He had done pioneering work in electricity, building a massive **electromagnet** and inventing an early form of telegraph. He went on to organize a group of volunteer weather observers, which later became the US Weather Bureau.

Joseph Henry's encouragement to Bell, at a critical stage of his work, was crucial to Bell's final success. Bell later repaid his debt to Henry by becoming a **trustee** of the Smithsonian and himself giving money to found its Astrophysical Laboratory.

Today the Smithsonian is in charge of many museums, galleries and research centres in the United States.

Joseph Henry, whose advice was crucial to Bell's success. Bell later repaid his generosity.

"Mr Watson, Come Here!"

Bell repeated his accidental discovery several times over to assure himself that it was no freak happening. Then he sketched out a design for the first electric speaking telephone and gave it to Watson to make. Watson had it ready for testing the following evening. It consisted of a wooden frame on which was mounted a sound receiver with a steel reed touching a tightly-stretched membrane of parchment.

When Watson spoke loudly into the telephone, Bell, in the next room, heard nothing. They changed places to take advantage of Bell's practised diction and Watson's super-sensitive hearing. Watson swore that he "could unmistakably hear the tones of his voice and almost catch a word now and then." But "almost" was not good enough. Much work remained to be done before the telephone could be introduced to the world.

Bell had another problem on his mind: Mabel Hubbard, who was now nearly eighteen. In June 1875, he wrote to Mrs Hubbard:–

"I have discovered that my interest in my dear pupil ... has ripened into a far deeper feeling ... I have learned to love her."

Mrs Hubbard pointed out how very young Mabel was and asked him to let the matter rest for a year. But Bell could not. A month later he wrote to Mabel, declaring his love. Eventually she was allowed to meet him alone, and she gave him some cause for hope, although she said she did not love him. Bell was elated nevertheless. It was, he recorded at the time, "the happiest day of my life." In September he went home to Brantford , exhausted by work and nervous strain.

Revived by his visit home, Bell returned to lecturing and working on the telephone, only to find himself in open conflict with Mabel's father, who wrote to him in angry terms:–

A man of property — at last. Bell in 1876, the year his invention was patented.

Bell's telephone: the same handset could be used to transmit or receive, but using two was easier.

"I have been sorry to see how little interest you seem to take in telegraph matters … Your whole course since you returned has been a very great disappointment to me, and a sore trial."

In the end, though Bell tried to make things up, they quarrelled openly and violently. But Bell and Mabel finally got engaged on Thanksgiving Day, 25 November.

In January 1876 Bell moved out of the Sanders' house in Salem and went to live in two rooms in the attic of a boarding-house at 5 Exeter Place, Boston. He made one of these rooms his workshop and worked frantically on perfecting the telephone transmitter and drawing up the detailed description of its working required by the Patent Office.

On the morning of 14 February, Mr Hubbard, acting on Bell's behalf, filed the telephone patent in Washington. A few hours later, on the same day, Elisha Gray, believing that he himself was about to be successful, filed a claim to warn off other inventors from attempting to make a telephone. But Bell had already beaten him to it. Over the following years, literally hundreds of lawsuits would be brought by Gray,

A pair of early Bell telephones, dated 1877.

into Bell's bedroom, where he stood waiting with his ear pressed to the receiver. "Almost at once I was astonished to hear Bell's voice … distinctly saying, 'Mr Watson, come here, I want you!' "

It was the first intelligible telephone conversation. Elated, Bell wrote to his father later that day, using these prophetic words:–

"I feel that … the day is coming when telegraph wires will be laid on to houses just like water or gas — and friends converse with each other without leaving home."

and others, to challenge Bell's patent. But in every case the courts upheld Bell's claim to be the only and original inventor of the telephone.

In March 1876, Bell sketched out a new apparatus for Watson to make. This consisted of a **diaphragm**, into which you spoke, making it vibrate. The vibration made a wire, attached to it, dip into a metal cup filled with water and acid. Different sounds would cause the wire to dip into the acid-water to varying degrees. This would alter the flow of electric current. The receiver would then turn this electric current back into sound — whether those noises were musical notes or human speech.

Watson, still working from Court Street, put together the new device in a matter of days and on 10 March 1876 brought it to Exeter Place for testing. The transmitter was set up in Bell's workshop and Watson went

The first model of the telephone approved for Post Office use.

Helen Keller

Helen Keller, born in Alabama in 1880, became one of the most famous people of her time. Tragically, a mysterious illness made her blind and deaf when she was only nineteen months old. Her despairing parents tried to bring her up but had great difficulty in communicating with her. Finally, when she was about six, they appealed to Bell for help, as he was the country's leading expert on the problems of the deaf.

Bell was delighted to assist and helped to arrange for Helen to be taught by Annie Sullivan, who became Helen's lifelong companion. Bell continued to be Helen's friend. When she was 21, he arranged a surprise holiday for her and Annie at Niagara Falls.

Helen Keller went on to devote her long life to raising funds for the blind and deaf. She once wrote about Bell:–

"You have always shown a father's joy in my successes and a father's tenderness when things have not gone right."

Helen Keller (left, seated) **with her lifelong teacher Annie Sullivan and Bell in 1894.**

An Emperor's Assistance

Bell had made a working telephone, but his struggle for success was not yet over. When, three days later, he arranged a demonstration for his business partner, Gardiner Hubbard, the apparatus produced only faint, unclear sounds. Hubbard tried to get Bell to go back to his original project:–

"If you could make one good invention in the telegraph, you would secure an annual income ... and then you could ... teach Visible Speech and experiment in telegraphy with an easy and undisturbed conscience."

Hubbard then found a more convincing argument. He persuaded his daughter Mabel to tell Bell that she would not marry him until he had successfully completed the telegraph experiments. Bell compromised by working hard at both telephone *and* telegraph. In an attempt to make the telephone transmitter more reliable, he went back to using electromagnets instead of the variable-resistance acid-water method. The electromagnet did give a more reliable transmission but with a very weak signal, so that the speaker had to shout.

Bell's next challenge was to get his invention known to the public. Years of demonstrations of Visible Speech had made him an accomplished public performer. He was not afraid

The Centennial Exhibition held in Philadelphia in 1876 — a celebration of American national pride.

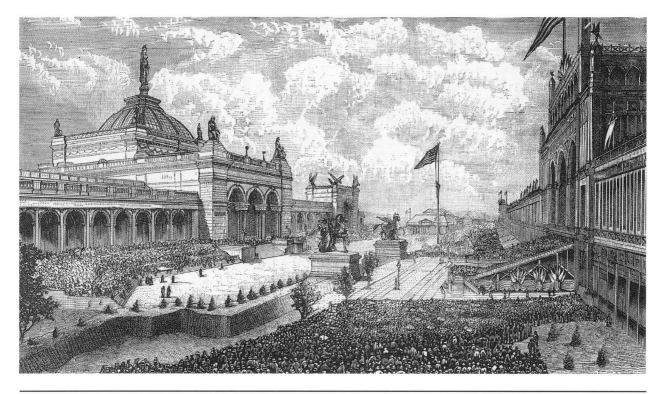

Pedro II (1825–91) Emperor of Brazil, whose interest gave Bell's invention instant fame.

of addressing large meetings, but first he had to find influential audiences who would listen to him.

In May 1876, Bell gave two lectures and a demonstration before groups of local scientists in Boston. They were impressed, but this was not the national publicity he wanted. Then came an unexpected opportunity which Bell was, at first, very reluctant to take.

The year 1876 marked the first hundred years of American independence and a massive exhibition was staged in Philadelphia to celebrate the event. It included exhibits of scientific achievements. Hubbard urged Bell to seize his chance to go and show off the telephone. Bell said he couldn't possibly spare the time because he had to mark examination papers and prepare a new university course. So Hubbard again got Mabel to plead with Bell, who finally gave in and agreed to go.

Bell's big moment came on June 25 when, by chance, Pedro II Emperor of Brazil, was visiting the exhibition. The Emperor had already met Bell while visiting the Boston School for the Deaf a few weeks earlier and had been very impressed with his work. He greeted Bell like an old friend and gladly took part in a demonstration of the new invention. Bell went to the far end of the huge exhibition hall and

began to recite Hamlet's famous speech "To be or not to be … " into the transmitter. He had scarcely begun when the Emperor, listening to the receiver at the other end of the hall, jumped out of his chair, exclaiming "I hear, I hear!" This royal amazement at once persuaded the learned scientists who were with him to try the telephone for themselves. The British inventor, Sir William Thomson, wrote in his report of the occasion that he was "astonished and delighted" at "perhaps the greatest marvel hitherto achieved by the electric telegraph."

Bell now went on to improve the range of the telephone. In August, at Paris, Ontario, he managed to hear words spoken by his father some distance away at Brantford. In

October, Bell and Watson carried out the first two-way conversation over outdoor wires, speaking from Boston to Cambridge, on opposite banks of the Charles River. In December they managed to transmit a message between Boston and North Conway, New Hampshire, over 225 km (140 miles) away; but the sound quality was still very poor.

People were beginning to take notice of Bell's invention but at first they misunderstood how it worked. In January 1877, the citizens of Boston were surprised to learn that a Japanese student of Bell's had spoken over the telephone to two of his fellow countrymen who were studying at Harvard University.

Apparently the telephone could even speak Japanese!

In February of that year the telephone chalked up another "first," when news of a lecture Bell was giving in Salem was telephoned to Watson and a reporter from the *Boston Globe* at 5 Exeter Place. This was the first use of the telephone in news reporting. In April, Watson and Bell managed to hold a conversation between Boston and New York, though again the sound quality was poor. This "call," like

A small gathering of Boston sceptics listening to Bell's speech relayed by telephone during a demonstration in 1877.

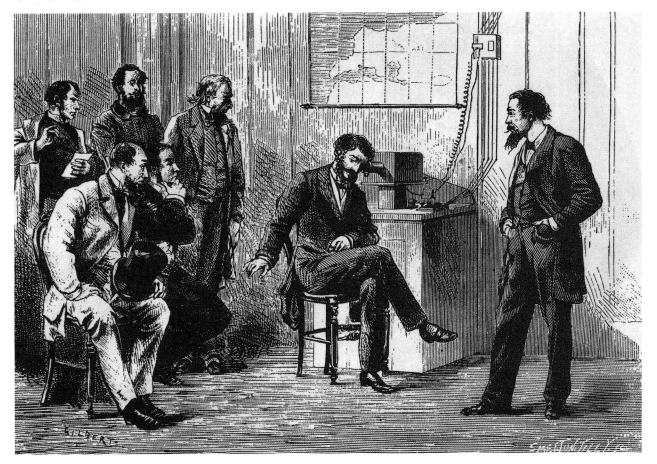

previous efforts at long-distance communication, was made by linking telephone apparatus with telegraph wires usually used to send messages in Morse code. The day after the Boston-New York link-up, another important milestone was reached — the installation of the world's first permanent outdoor telephone wire. This ran from Mr Williams' Court Street electrical shop to his home about 5 km (3 miles) away. In May, the first telephones were rented for business use, by a young banker who wanted a link between his office and his home.

In the same month, Gardiner Hubbard issued the first advertisement for a telephone. His claims for its efficiency were, however, very cautious:

"The proprietors of the Telephone ... are now prepared to furnish Telephones for the transmission of articulate speech through instruments not more than twenty miles apart ... Conversation can easily be carried on after slight practice and with occasional repetition of a word or sentence ... after a few trials the ear becomes accustomed to the peculiar sound ... "

Meanwhile Bell and Watson were busily promoting more public interest in their new technology by giving a series of spectacular public demonstrations throughout the cities of the north-eastern United States. Bell would sit on the stage of a lecture hall with a phone beside him and three or four others linked to it placed around the hall. Watson,

accompanied by a small band, would then call in from somewhere between 8–40 km (5–25 miles) away and bellow "Yankee Doodle" or "Auld Lang Syne" down the wire, with shrill musical backing. Audiences were dumb-founded, awed and even a little afraid. A Providence newspaper said it sounded like the work of the Devil himself, and even the *New York Herald* found it "almost supernatural".

On 9 July 1877 the Bell Telephone Company was set up. Sanders, Hubbard and Mabel were major **shareholders**. Two days later, Alexander Graham Bell and Mabel were at last married. In August they sailed for England.

An illustrated magazine explains in detail the construction of Bell's telephone and the principles of its operation. Figs. 1 and 2 show the basic experimental version; 3, the "office" model; 4 and 5, the "portable"; 6, shows it in use.

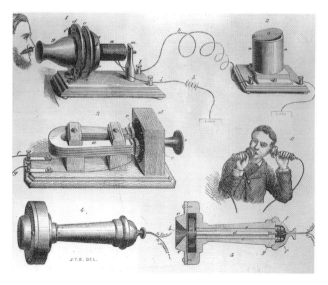

The Telephone Comes of Age

The first business use of the telephone began in May 1877. The first telephone exchange, linking telephones together, came into service in New Haven, Connecticut, in the following year. After this, exchanges were opened in many parts of the United States.

In March 1880, there were 138 US exchanges with 30,000 subscribers (telephone owners). By 1887 this had increased to a total of 150,000 subscribers in the United States and 26,000 in the United Kingdom. These were then the two major telephone-using countries in the world. (By 1982, there were 486 *million* telephones in the world.)

For some years, telephones were so expensive that only the rich could afford them. In the United Kingdom in the 1880s it cost £20 to have a phone installed — which in those days was as much as a servant earned in a whole year.

Below: **Women telephone operators in The National Telephone Company, about 1900.** Overleaf: **phoning from a train in the United States, 1907.**

Statesman of Science

In England, Bell demonstrated the telephone to Queen Victoria, who pronounced it "most extraordinary". He remained in Europe for over a year, introducing his young wife to the beauties of France, giving a course of lectures at Oxford and helping to found a day school for the deaf at Greenock in his native Scotland. He also had time to write a pamphlet for a group of London businessmen anxious to raise money for a telephone service in Britain. This contained a remarkably accurate prediction of how the use of the telephone would be developed over the next 50 years.

When Bell returned to Boston he tried to get involved in the new company but he had little interest in business and longed to get back to experimenting. His true feeling showed when he learned that Thomas Edison had invented a working phonograph (gramophone). Bell was infuriated that he had not done so himself. In 1880 he finally resigned from the Bell Telephone Company. By now he was a millionaire and entirely free to follow his own interests.

The year of Bell's resignation was marked by a new and unexpected

Edison recording his voice on his prototype gramophone.

honour. The French government awarded him the Volta Prize for science, worth a large sum of money. Bell used the prize to set up the Volta Laboratory in Washington, devoted to scientific research. In 1883 he went on, with the support of Gardiner Hubbard, to rescue the ailing magazine *Science* and help turn it into the important scientific journal that it still is today.

Bell continued to work tirelessly on many inventions. At the Volta Laboratory he worked on a "photophone", a device for transmitting speech, not over a wire but over a ray of light. At the time this had no practical use; nowadays it is recognized as a forerunner of modern achievements in fibre optics.

Another of his remarkable inventions was the induction balance, a device which could be used to locate metal objects in the body. This was first used when the US President James Garfield was shot by an assassin's bullet in 1881. The bullet lodged in the President's

Learning to speak at the Deaf and Dumb Institute, London, 1908.

back so deeply that it could not be found. Bell tried to locate it electrically, but the President died before he could do so.

Bell did not patent any of these inventions. He simply gave them away for the common good. Bell's interest in Edison's gramophone led him to work with other scientists at the Volta Laboratory. Together they developed a device for recording music, better types of record (both flat and cylindrical) and a superior "reproducer" on which to play the records. These inventions were patented in 1886 and the patents sold to the American Graphophone Company. The proceeds went to convert the Volta Laboratory into the Volta Bureau for the Promotion of the Teaching of Speech to the Deaf. When this was established in 1890, Bell was elected as its

Bell (centre) **at the opening of the New York–San Francisco line, 1915.**

president. He also gave a large amount of his money to support its work. The following year he gave the Smithsonian Institution enough money to set up an astrophysical laboratory.

Bell's concern for the deaf led him to take an interest in **genetics**, the study of how we inherit characteristics from our parents. He was especially interested in the way some people inherit deafness. He also conducted experiments with sheep-breeding at his summer home on Cape Breton Island, off the north-east coast of Nova Scotia.

The other major passion of his life, however, was flying. He encouraged and helped to finance the ill-fated flying experiments of Samuel P. Langley, the secretary of the Smithsonian Institution. He also made experiments of his own. Out of these came another invention — the **tetrahedral** kite. In 1907 he set up

the Aerial Experiment Association, and became its president.

Bell's wide-ranging interests also made him president of the National Geographic Society and a governor of the Smithsonian Institution. He was awarded honorary degrees and medals by the world's greatest universities, among them Harvard, Oxford, Edinburgh and Heidelberg.

Bell holding a model of his tetrahedral kite, 1903.

Bell enjoying a vigorous old age and his grandson's company.

His enthusiasm for scientific work remained undimmed even in old age. During World War I he invented a **hydrofoil** — a high-speed motorboat that could reach speeds of over 112 kph (70 mph). In 1915 he inaugurated the first transcontinental telephone line from New York to San Francisco — with Watson replying from the San Francisco end. Bell's first words were "Mr Watson, are you there?" They had made great advances since the day, 39 years earlier, when Bell had first summoned Watson to his room in such a remarkable way!

In 1917 the Governor-General of Canada unveiled a memorial to celebrate the invention of the telephone at Brantford , Ontario, where the Bells had lived. The family home there was dedicated as a public park.

Bell with H.P. McNeil, maker of these hydrofoil models based on Bell's designs.

Five years later, on 2 August 1922, Alexander Graham Bell died, aged 75. On the day of his funeral, he was honoured by a unique gesture. As his body was lowered into a tomb cut into the top of a mountain on Cape Breton Island, every telephone in North America observed a minute's silence.

The great American inventor, Thomas Edison, paid tribute to him as:

"My late friend, Alexander Graham Bell, whose world-famed invention annihilated time and space, and brought the human family in closer touch."

Right: **Bell and his wife Mabel on Cape Breton Island, 1909.**

Find Out More ...

Important Dates

1847 3 March, Alexander Graham Bell born in Edinburgh, Scotland

1863 Teaches at Elgin

1866 Teaches in Bath

1868-70 Studies at University College, London

1870 Emigrates with parents to Canada

1871 Teaches Visible Speech system in Boston, USA

1872 Takes on own deaf pupils

1873 Appointed Professor at Boston University

1874 Begins experiments to make a telephone

1875 First transmission of sound by telephone

1876 First transmission of speech by telephone, and Bell obtains patent for such
Public demonstration given at the Philadelphia Centennial Exhibition

1877 Establishment of the Bell Telephone Company
Marries Mabel Hubbard

1878 Spends a year in the UK

1880 Resigns from the Bell Telephone Company
Wins Volta Prize and sets up Volta Laboratory

1882 Becomes a US citizen

1883 Re-establishes *Science* magazine

1886 Patents gramophone improvements

1890 Sets up American Association for the Promotion of Teaching of Speech to the Deaf

1891 Sets up Astrophysical Laboratory at the Smithsonian Institution

1896 Elected President of the National Geographic Society

1907 Founds Aerial Experiment Association

1915 Opens first transcontinental telephone line, from New York to San Francisco

1922 2 August, dies at his home on Cape Breton Island

Useful Information

Alexander Graham Bell Association for the Deaf and Hard of Hearing
AG Bell
3417 Volta Place, NW
Washington, DC 20007
USA
www.agbell.org

The Telephone Museum
McConnell Drive
Wolverton, Milton Keynes
MK12 5EL
www.mkheritage.co.uk/ttm

Useful Websites

Science Magazine
www.sciencemag.org

Smithsonian Institution
www.si.edu

Glossary

Diaphragm   In a telephone, a thin disc that vibrates when sound hits it.

Electromagnet   A piece of metal made magnetic by winding a coil of wire around it and passing electricity through the wire.

Genetics   The study of genes: how living things inherit characteristics from earlier generations.

Hydrofoil   A boat fitted underneath with a blade on which it can travel at high speed.

Larynx   The back of the throat, where speech sounds are made.

Membrane   A thin sheet of skin or similar material.

Patent   An official document which gives an inventor the right to his or her invention so that nobody else can copy it.

Patent Office   The office where patents are registered.

Scarlet fever   An infectious illness, once common, that gave you a sore throat and rash and could do lasting damage, such as making people deaf.

Shareholders   People who own a company and have shares in the money it makes.

Sign language   A way of communicating that does not use speech.

Symbols   Patterns or pictures that have special meanings: e.g. a roadsign showing a white arrow on a blue background is a symbol meaning that traffic can go in only one direction in that street.

Telegraph   A way of sending messages along wires, using electricity. The telegraph could not send the sounds of the human voice, so operators had to use codes to send messages. Morse code, using dots and dashes, was often used.

Tetrahedral   A solid geometric shape with four faces (a cube has six faces).

Tuberculosis   A once-common disease that produced growths in the lungs, and was often fatal. It is also known as TB.

Tuning fork   A pronged metal instrument that gives off a particular note when struck. It is used to tune musical instruments.

Vowel   A type of speech sound: in English these sounds are written as a, e, i, o and u.

Index

Picture Acknowledgements

The publishers would like to thank the following for their kind permission to reproduce their photographs in this book:
E.T. Archive 28 (bottom), 29; Library of Congress 4,5,7 (top), 10,18; The Mansell Collection, frontispiece, 9,15,27 (top); Mary Evans Picture Library, cover, 8,11,12,13,14,19,24,25,27 (bottom), 28 (top); Radio Times Hulton Picture Library 20,22,23,26 (bottom); The Science Museum 16,17 (top); Wayland Picture Library 17 (bottom), 21,26 (top).